The Wars & Other Related Events

Books by R.M. West

Revisionist historical writings

The Germane

A nationalist trilogy

The Nation as Race and Myth

The Revolt Against Empire

The Wars & Other Related Events

For those who still seek the desideratum

THE WARS
& OTHER
RELATED
EVENTS

A Political Novel

by R.M. West

○ ○ ○ **O**
4 Moons Press

Seattle

The Wars & Other Related Events

Cover art and design by Peter West and Anita Evans.

*

Contents

Foreword

What is history? Most often it is the tricked-out fiction of those who control a society.

After the Second World War Winston Churchill was asked how he expected to be judged by history.

"Very highly," he replied, "I am writing it."

Revisionist historians have argued, however, that Churchill's notorious appetite for war and glory had cost Britain its empire.

You are holding in your hand the third book of a political trilogy. These fictional histories describe two opposing world views that could eventually breed war.

Such wars and their related events might never take place, but if they do, they would probably look much like this....

R.M.W.

The Wars & Other Related Events

PART ONE

This is my morning: rise up now, rise up, great noontide! Thus spoke Zarathustra and left his cave, glowing and strong, like a morning sun emerging from behind dark mountains.

—Nietzsche, Thus Spoke Zarathustra

1

Whether it was by coincidence, or intention, I received an e-mail on the fourteenth of February, which happened to be my seventieth birthday—a personal milestone of sorts that earlier in my life I would not have expected to reach. Yes, I am now an old man, but still at my fighting weight and, unless the weather is stormy, I can be seen (even in February) taking my usual two-mile walk on a sloping trail, ornamented with several small waterfalls, that rises above the rustic outskirts of the Swiss town of Davos and an unpretentious condominium, converted from an early 20th century sanitarium, which is where I have my home.

The e-mail in question had been sent by a Dominic Putnam. It was just the latest of a number of such messages I received from him in resent months. He had identified himself as a writer of contemporary political history, who was attempting to meet with the surviving founders of the Movement that led to a successful anti-globalist Revolution several decades earlier. Using my standard negative reply to his requests for an interview, I reminded him that the historical ground he wished us to visit had already been visited on countless occasions by others at least as knowledgeable on the subject as was I—and that any additional contribution I might make to the existing myth would be only a wasteful redundancy. Then embarking upon what must be described as a shameless diversionary tactic, I mentioned once again my recently awakened interest in the social structure of ant colonies, the pursuit of which was requiring most of my rapidly dwindling reservoir of time and energy.

The following is an excerpt from this most recent e-mail from Dominic Putnam, in which he referred to my current interest in the study of ants:

Again congratulations on your foray into the study of a completely alien society from our own: the society of ants! This only highlights the plain fact that age in terms of years is quite relative especially when we are dealing with remarkable persons. Who would have guessed that a man of action like yourself, who has spent most of his career dealing with the "sturm und drang" of our own complicated society, has at the present time undertaken a critical investigation of the societal complexities of insects—or to be more species-specific, in myrmecology, the study of ants.

(Your humble correspondent found that Greek-rooted word in Google.) But now permit me to introduce a rather mundane fact to the remaining contents of this e-mail: I will luckily be spending some time in your majestic area of the Alps during the last week of February, and wonder if we might have a brief chat at that time….

My reply to this e-mail was immediate and direct:

Unfortunately, I expect to be away then.

2

On a gloomy evening about a week later, I was flipping through the pages of a recent issue of The Economist magazine in the glass-enclosed community room and library located on one side of the condominium's quiet lobby. I was not, however, concerned with any financial matter of the moment, I was simply wondering where I would have dinner that evening.

Straight across the lobby (where the dining room of the former sanitarium had once been) was now the elegant Edelweiss Restaurant, with likenesses of the hardy mountain flower etched in the frosted glass of its entrance doors, and where excellent Swiss Alpine cuisine was featured—while in my plainly decorated apartment on the floor above was what remained of yesterday's pot of *dol bot*, a native Himalayan vegetable stew that I cook and consume with the great gusto of an aspiring vegan almost every evening. And so, as I idly scanned the pages of the

Economist magazine, the question of dinner was evolving in my mind from *where* would I dine to *what* would my dinner be: a robust Alpine omelet with all the trimmings, or a rather austere bowl of left-over lentils, white marrow beans, wilted greens and rice?....

It was then that a nondescript young man, wearing a mustard-color coat and long gray scarf, entered the tranquil lobby from the evening gloom, and leaning determinedly forward, as if he were still outside struggling against a wintry wind, made his way to a directory on the wall next to the elevator. Just moments later the young man pressed one of the buzzer keys—there was no response. He immediately repeated the process and was again met with the same result. Then glancing around the lobby, he eventually noticed me seated comfortably beside the dancing blue and red flames of a gas heated fireplace on the other side of the community room's glass wall. As our eyes met I knew who this young man was—I somehow knew that this was *Dominic Putnam*, and no one else....

Many years earlier, at the very beginning of the Civil War, when members of the Revolutionary Coordinating Council were preparing to go under cover, a brave young woman gave me a small nickel-plated pistol engraved with a crisscross design on its polished bone handle. This diminutive weapon had an almost effeminate, toy-like appearance, although I would soon learn that it was quite deadly. I lost contact with this daring woman during the wartime chaos that followed, but I did manage to hold onto the pistol. And now, as this young man approached, I instinctively shifted my weight slightly and brushed a hand against the weapon resting discreetly under my tweed jacket. Yes, I still carry a gun in 2039, not because of the persistent threat of Islamic terrorism that seemingly lurks at every doorpost, or the increasingly aggressive behavior of the current Arab Caliphate installed just beyond our eastern borders, but because there are members of our own nation that still consider persons with my political history as deserving of payback. Despite the random threats, however, I have refused to withdraw from the *public square* as other members of the Movement have reluctantly, or even eagerly, done. Most afternoons I continue to make a point of visiting my favorite café down in the village, where I order a usual bitterly strong cup of Swiss coffee from one of the pretty waitresses, who still seem to enjoy my good-natured banter, and then I spend an hour or so perusing the English language newspapers displayed on the rack. Although this little gun has not always prevented the nuisance of dealing with an occasional wannabe *provocateur*, I like to think that its rumored presence on my person has probably prevented more violent incidents to occur....

The young man, seemingly somewhere in his

late twenties, who I intuitively presumed was none other than Dominic Putnam, had in the meantime resolutely crossed the lobby, hesitated at the entrance to the community room, then quietly opened the door and cautiously entered.

"Please excuse me," he said with a slight unidentifiable accent. "Would you happen to know if the person in 217 is away?"

"Yes, I would," I replied. "He is not. He expected to be away at this time, but his plans were changed."

"That's fortunate," said the young man. "I was hoping to see him."

"Well, you are looking at him now," I said, removing my glasses and placing The Economist magazine on the chair next to me.

"You are?...."

"I am," I said.

3

Yes, this young man was, indeed, Dominic Putnam. He was staying not far from the railway station down the hill in Davos—staying, he said, with a touch of gravity, in a bed-and-breakfast that is reached only by crossing a gushing mountain stream on a wobbly wooden foot-bridge located just north of the village.

Dominic Putnam did not depart that evening until I had reluctantly agreed to meet with him the following afternoon in Davos. (My favorite café is The Summit, I told him. It was not very far from the infamous wooden foot-bridge that he had spoken of.) When he finally ventured into the fog again, I returned to my apartment and prepared to reheat the left-over *dol bot* I had mentioned earlier—refreshing it with what still remained of an over-ripe beefsteak tomato, an extra large clove of finely chopped garlic and an additional generous pinch of curry. Following a telecast of the BBC evening news, I made a double martini with some premium Russian vodka I had been hoarding in my liquor cabinet until something happened that was worth celebrating. The *something* that evening was the fate of a flotilla of Saracen slave ships that was intercepted earlier in the day off the south-eastern coast of Sicily by elements of the European Naval Coastal Command. There they were on the television screen for all the world to see: the captured Arab raiding vessels lying dead in the water, and the liberated hostages scrambling onto the decks of the European gunboats. The narrator concluded this report by saying:

The Islamic Jihad will ultimately be crushed by the united will of European Whites....

The next afternoon I found Dominic Putnam already seated at a window table in The Summit Café with a bright new mechanical pencil and an open notebook in readiness.

"Well, where shall we start?" I said to him a bit impatiently, after ordering coffee.

At this stage of my life, I have grown rather intolerant of people who mindlessly attempt to insert themselves into my routines—malleable as those routines might appear to be to the casual observer. At times, when I feel especially intruded upon, I am reminded of the opening lines in Cakes and Ale, an early twentieth century novel by the then highly popular English writer Somerset Maugham, in which the main character of the story complains to the reader:

I have noticed that when someone asks for you on the telephone and, finding you out, leaves a message begging you to call him up the moment you come in, and it's important, the matter is more often important to him than to you....

Dominic Putnam certainly understood by now that exhuming the political past was not something I looked forward to doing. However, this seemed not to have dampened his enthusiasm for the projected interview with me, even if it was only to be for an hour. From the start it was evident that he wanted to talk particularly about the wars: the 2013-17 Civil War bred by the anti-globalist Revolution, the failed 2019-20 Chinese inspired counter-secessionist invasion of the Continent and the still unresolved, millennium-long Arab Islamic Jihad against the European White world that had been resumed in September 2001. Dominic Putnam was soon quoting the famous von Clausewitz maxim: *War is the continuation of politics by other means.* Yes, war would certainly remain a universal reality, I thought, remembering that I had made this same comment aloud quite recently (although it was addressed only to myself), as I imagined seeing a mass of regimented ants marching off to war—the only thing missing from their miniature enactment of martial discipline being a gaudy array of battle flags. Dominic Putnam had attempted (unnecessarily, I thought) to buttress the continuing relevance of the Clausewitz dictum by making the claim that the only political event of any lasting significance in America during the entire nineteenth century was the bloody civil war fought during the 1860s between the Northern and Southern states over the question of States' Rights....

This assertion prompted me to remind him, perhaps a bit too sternly, that our one hour interview was limited to a discussion of twenty-first century events.

And so the door was promptly slammed shut on any discussion of wars other than our own twenty-first century Civil War, the unsuccessful Chinese-led intervention against the European secession and the Arab Islamic Caliphate's most recently resumed Jihad against the Occident, that was begun in September of 2001. The Great Recession, that began in the autumn of 2008, and the seismic First European Nationalist International, which took place at Moscow in early April of 2012, were two other closely related events linked to the wars themselves.

In the course of discussing the initial phases of our Revolution and Civil War, Dominic Putnam brought up the now rarely heard name of Lorenz Ehrenstaat. The dialogue then continued something like this:

"Would you say that Lorenz Ehrenstaat was a core member of the anti-globalist Movement?" He asked.

"Yes, he was one of its founders."

"Some of the other founding members have said that he was a controversial figure."

"Lorenz Ehrenstaat is no longer able to speak for himself. It would be difficult for me to pass judgment on him now."

"He was criticized at a raucous meeting held in the Baltic city of Lubeck during an early period of the Civil War."

"A doctrinal dispute was taking place during that time."

"I was told that you rebuked Lorenz Ehrenstaat at the meeting in Lubeck."

"*Rebuked*, is a strong word."

"Several of the surviving founders have used that word."

"The meeting at Lubeck was called to affirm a principle, which had become a corner stone of the anti-globalist Movement."

"Could you briefly describe the substance of that founding principle?"

"The meeting confirmed that our movement

was based upon European White identity—that the criterion of our nationhood was our race."

"Did he question that criterion?"

"At that December 2014 meeting in Lubeck Lorenz Ehrenstaat had spoken of *geography as our destiny.*"

"And you rebuked him for placing geography in the preeminent place above race?"

"Yes, I would say that is what happened...."

4

While walking back to my apartment after the talk with Dominic Putnam in The Summit Café, I reflected briefly on my life as an eye witness to the near death and then the sudden resurgence of the European White world. Before the successful anti-globalist Revolution, the secularists had been busily dismantling the spiritual as well as the physical component of our mythos, and White racial pride had become déclassé after the total defeat of Europe in 1945. In addition, the barely recognizable remnants of sovereign European political will had created a perfect storm of confusion in the minds of authentic Europeans throughout the Continent, as well as in America—while at the same time this obvious White bewilderment was being celebrated as enlightened tolerance by the self-hating European secularists, the invading foreign migrants and the Arab jihad terrorists. (Remarkably, during this same pre-revolutionary period, it was only the recently freed European east that was creating a bulwark, a locus of defiance to threats from secularism, the wave of foreign migrants and the militant Arab Islamic Caliphate....)

Dusk was falling as I approached the curving drive leading up to the silvery, streamlined building that housed my rather Spartan, but quite adequate quarters. Windows were beginning to glow behind the low deck railings of its two-story façade—while the condominium's fanciful ensign, a scarlet griffin on a purple field dotted with daisies, was catching gusts of wind from its pole beside the main entrance.

My conversation with Dominic Putnam had lasted longer than the allotted one hour. Its length had been almost double that, and I was tired after it was over—so, instead of starting to prepare my dinner, I took a nap. When I awoke an hour or so later, I brewed some strong coffee, made an extra thick cheddar cheese sandwich—and then removed my computer from the bottom drawer of my desk, along with a cigar box, which incredibly still contained a small collection of my boyhood treasures: a prized iridescent peewee marble, a blue, gray and white kingfisher feather, an Indian-head penny, a bent Roman *denarius*, a shiny tin badge from a political convention engraved with a rampant dragon and Chinese calligraphy. The underside of the cigar box lid was decorated with a multi-colored, embossed portrait of a young woman wearing a winged helmet and body armor appropriate for a Valkyrie, or Joan of Arc. In one hand she carried a sword, with the other she held aloft a pennant bearing a single word: *Fidelity*. How, or why this common little wooden cigar box had followed me around most of my life remained a personal mystery. Perhaps it held a good-luck charm of some sort that I had not yet recognized. In any case, this enigmatic box had also become the place where I now stashed my computer flash drives for the deliberately sketchy (coded) journal that I had begun to keep while serving as a member of the Revolutionary Coordinating Council at the beginning of the Revolution. On this particular evening I removed a flash drive from the box whose identifying label contained dates that were inclusive of entries I had made in my journal during the decisive month of December 2014:

12 December 2014

The doctrinal question that was posed by Lorenz Ehrenstaat has been successfully dealt with! This was an extremely important matter. A major crack in the philosophical foundation of a new revolutionary movement such as our own almost always proves to be fatal. At this lively meeting in the city of Lubeck, I did not attack Lorenz Ehrenstaat personally, I did not attempt to belittle him—I simply pointed out the major errors in his argument. It would be arrogant to say that I felt the weight of history bearing down on my shoulders as I engaged Lorenz Ehrenstaat in this basic ideological dispute. On the other hand, there had been an undeniable atmosphere of historical importance in the crowded hall that evening. And, unfortunately, afterward there were puddles of metaphorical blood left on the floor, as well.

Edward Schmieder, one of the earliest and perhaps the most resolute founders of the anti-globalist Movement, had compared this confrontation in Lubeck to the biblical collision of Peter and Paul at Antioch, when Paul rebuked Peter for requiring the newly Christianized Gentiles to accept Jewish law. The deeply religious artist El Greco painted this confrontational scene at least three times. It seems that this devout painter from the island of Crete could not quite persuade himself that he had captured the kernel of the colossal moment, the essence of the instant, when these two beleaguered men, these proto-Christians found themselves locked in this historic conflict—especially Paul the outlier from Tarsus, the grim-faced convert from orthodox Judaism, the plagued, yet unyielding challenger of Peter his divinely appointed leader....

5

Now here we are again in the current year of 2039—almost twenty-five years after my debate with Lorenz Ehrenstaat over the relative importance of race and geography in the future of our then incipient political Movement. It was an impassioned argument clothed in language that was not always eloquent, but whose words were meant to be transparently honest. A debate that was followed just days later by the tragic death of Lorenz Ehrenstaat. I am now an old man of seventy, who even at this age is purposely armed with something more reliable and compelling than mere words—and who still frequently broods over what seems to have been a grotesquely inflated price levied by fate upon a fallible, but honorable man for losing a verbal dispute—for losing a less than glorious scuffle of words! Good God! An absolute phalanx of raised hands and the confirming thunder of a chairman's gavel in a crowded Lubeck meeting hall on a dark December night in 2014—was all of that not sufficient salt for the wounds inflicted upon this upright, but mistaken man?....

Ludwig Wittgenstein, a brilliant philosopher of language, addressed the many difficulties found in the practical use of words. He said these linguistic difficulties arise mostly from the misunderstanding of the physical logic of words. For example, his Picture theory works only when the proposition is pictured as an actual fact, not as a supposition. Perhaps this was Wittgenstein's way of saying, 'That is how it is—so deal with it.' He offered humorous as well as serious examples of some misunderstandings that are caused by the careless, or improper use of words. *I'll keep it in mind.* This should not be confused with *I'll keep it in a box.* And he boldly faced the ultimate failure of language while his associates were purposefully looking the other away. He explored the deep dark terrain of the unutterable, the inexpressible, those shadowy places in language that vex the fussy, nit-picking theoretician. In his only published work *Tractatus Logico-Philosophicus* he addressed that which truly lies beyond the reach of words—the yawning, the bottomless, the ineffable—and he wrote this unforgettable, almost mystical line in closing:

Whereof one cannot speak, thereof one must be silent.

The Wars & Other Related Events

I have not formally studied Wittgenstein, nor have I read his *Tractatus Logico-Philosophicus*. I did not stumble on his name in some obscure footnote. (Possible footnote: the *son of an* ultra-*rich Viennese armaments dealer, who as a young man deliberately gave away all of his inherited wealth.*) I did not happen upon the name of Ludwig Wittgenstein in some small, hard to read, obscure addendum. I was introduced to the name of this maverick philosopher of language by a brilliant Russian *military* officer whom I interviewed in the Italian city of Bologna during the early autumn of 2015....

6

What follows is an excerpt from a long entry in my journal describing a conversation I had with Nicholas Abelov, a young anti-globalist military commander after his victory over a counter-secessionist army in central Italy.

28 September 2015
As a member of the Coordinating Council, I recently visited the Italian city of Bologna to assess the current military situation in central Italy with a young, charismatic field commander, Col. Nicholas Abelov. He had just concluded a brilliantly led campaign in the Apennine Mountains northwest of Bologna, where an entire globalist French-Arab army had surrendered to his pan-European force. Nicholas Abelov was born in January 1990, and at the still youthful age of twenty-five, he has become the most successful commander of anti-globalist troops presently fighting in Europe. In the spring of 2013, at the beginning of the Revolution

and Civil War, Nicholas Abelov, along with a number of fellow university students, volunteered to serve in an anti-globalist infantry brigade that was being formed in St. Petersburg. Then, quite remarkably, after just a matter of months he was in command of several brigades that were clearing the Crimean Peninsula and the important Black Sea port of Sevastopol, of an outlaw army of Khazars that had earlier gained control of the major waterways in southern Ukraine, the Crimean region and much of south-western Russia...

I had my talk with Col. Abelov in a quiet archive reading room off the gilded and ornately furnished Renaissance library of the University of Bologna. When I finally found him alone in the reading room (we had not been specific as to where we would meet in the palatial library), I was surprised to see that this brilliant field commander was dressed in the plain, yellowish khaki uniform of a common soldier without insignia of rank, or any military decoration other than the "Ring of Thunder" badge pinned over his heart that was worn by all anti-globalist soldiers, regardless of rank, who had been in close combat with the enemy—yes, he was quite alone there in the reading room, sitting at a table with a sheet of architectural drawing paper lying before him, upon which he was adding details to a pencil sketch he had just made of the very building in which we were to have our meeting, the nonpareil Archiginnasio palace library: just two stories high with a series of gracefully imposing porticos facing the chapel of Santa Maria dei Bulgari in the Piazza Galvani....

"Col. Nicholas Abelov, I presume!" I said, somewhat theatrically, as I approached the table at which he was sitting—and I was immediately startled by the sound of my own voice as it echoed from the lofty ceiling of the formerly silent reading room. Col. Abelov stood up with a friendly smile and we shook hands, then he gestured to a chair just across the narrow table from his.

"This is my favorite building in Bologna," he said, holding up the sketch, so that I could see the striking exterior lines of the Archiginnasio palace library. "It would certainly be a great tragedy if this building were to be destroyed in a war."

"A tragedy, indeed," I said.

"Would you say that the major materials of the library's facade are sandstone and terracotta?" he asked.

"Yes, I would say, sandstone and terracotta," I said. (Who would have questioned the opinion of an obvious polymath, whose knowledge of architecture would have extended far beyond my own?)

"But we did not meet here to talk about Italian Renaissance architecture, did we?" he said with a gesture of cheerful resignation, and he placed his

sketch aside.

"Yes, sadly, we are here to talk about war," I said. "And I want to start by congratulating you on your brilliant victory over the French and Arabs in the Apennines."

"My troops should get all the accolades," he said. "They were superb."

"This defeat of globalist forces here in central Italy is only the most recent of your victories as a field commander, Col. Abelov. You certainly deserve some of that praise, as well."

"I had not been trained as a soldier," he replied, "but I quickly realized that in a revolution you must, more or less, learn by doing. I was actually trained in semantics at the university in St. Petersburg; the study of language, the ever changing meaning of words and the complicated relationship of words and symbols. A philosopher of language, Ludwig Wittgenstein, cautioned us to use words with care because words are truly slippery entities. They have the very unstable traits of quicksilver and the mysterious attributes of subatomic particles that apparently change their shape under the force of our gaze— a discovery made, I believe, by Max Planck during the formulation of his theory of Quantum Mechanics. Even now, modern semantics has challenged ancient principles of logic, arcane Aristotelian proposals, such as nothing can be both

not-x and x.... During my study of language, I discovered two figures that were to have a profound influence on how I perceived the world. The first, as I have just mentioned, Ludwig Wittgenstein whose poetic sensibility allowed him to delve more deeply than most into the mysteries of words. The second was another philosopher, the much misunderstood and maligned Friedrich Nietzsche, a great re-definer of our vocabulary, who used an entirely new lexicon to describe reality for us. Nietzsche called himself a Good European, and also thought of himself as a musician. He intuitively treated history's rhythms as music, and so discovered its symphonic leitmotifs. What is more, he heard in history's music not one universal melody, but a symphony of many diverse melodies. His was a musician's sense of history's oceanic cadences that mimic the tides and the flights of the spheres in the heavens. He recognized that each human culture was of a certain time and place, appearing and then vanishing, in the way the moon comes into view and then disappears again during the Earth's celestial journey. With the clarity of intuition Nietzsche found in the tracks of the planets history's supreme theme: Eternal Recurrence, personified by his greatest literary creation the prophet Zarathustra, Nietzsche's representation of history itself clothed in human form....

"But we have not yet turned our attention to

the subject that brought us together here in the first place, the topic represented by that clanging, single-syllable, ancient Anglo-Saxon word—war. By the beginning of 2013, it was clear that there would soon be a civil war. And being completely untrained as a soldier, I proceeded to give myself a crash-course in practical military instruction by studying the writings of three soldiers who have been celebrated for their prowess in making war. The first was the writings of a Chinese, Sun Tzu, who lived in the fifth century B.C. and wrote a treatise on warfare that is still read today titled The Art of War. The second was Julius Caesar's highly praised Commentaries On the Gallic War, which curiously was written by Caesar in the third person, and was obviously meant by him to be an instructional work. The third was the military memoirs of Ulysses Grant, a soldier bearing a given name borrowed from the heroic myths of Homer, who was destined to become the victorious commander in the world's first modern war—the long and bloody nineteenth century civil war between the American northern and southern states….

*   "I prefaced my notes on the writings of these three soldiers with a quotation I had discovered earlier by Hesiod an eighth century B.C. Greek poet:*

*   'This man, I say, is most perfect who shall have understood everything for himself, after having devised*

what may be best afterward and unto the end.'

"One of the most enlightening facts I gleaned from my study of these three illustrious soldiers was their shared recognition of the great importance of waterways in developing battle plans. Yes, even now in this era of drone aircraft and other electronic forms of weaponry, nature's rivers still remain an important element in the planning and execution of military tactics. Sun Tzu counseled us bluntly: 'After crossing a river, you should get far away from it.' Julius Caesars' Commentaries on the Gallic War are filled with references to such major rivers as the Moselle, the Rhine, the Seine, etc.—and the Roman commander's fateful decision made on the banks of the Rubicon is certainly proverbial. Another example of the continued importance of rivers in modern military operations is Grant's decisive capture, after a long siege, of the strategic river port of Vicksburg, Mississippi, which cut the Southern Confederacy in two and guaranteed the North's eventual victory in the American Civil War. Since assuming the grave responsibilities of a field commander, I have made it an iron-clad rule to consult a topographical map of a region's waterways whenever I plan the movement of troops."

At that point, Col. Abelov picked up the pencil sketch he had made of the Archiginnasio palace, and turning over the sheet of paper to its blank side, he drew a rough circle—then quickly placed lines within the circle and filled the areas between the series of lines with shading.

"Now," he said, holding up the sheet of paper again, "let us imagine that this is a poorly drawn map of a battlefront on the Continent, not a sliced-up wheel of Swiss cheese. Europe is traversed by many rivers. Our opponents have continued to lose control of the territory lying between these river systems. During our action in the Apennine Mountains the Pannaro and the Santerno rivers were our allies—yes, we have learned to make allies of our rivers. Since the surrender of the French-Arab army group that was trapped between the rivers in the Apennines, I can confidently say that the globalist threat here in central Italy has become a thing of the past...."

7

The Civil War began in earnest early in 2013, following an incident, (now generally known as the *Strasbourg Outrage*) which had taken place in that city the previous September. The event resulted in the killing of scores of peaceful demonstrators by an armored unit of the French Mobile Guard, consisting of black African mercenaries from the former French African colony of Senegal.

On a sunny morning in September 2012, an orderly group of several thousand mostly youthful European Whites had begun a peaceful march from the campus of the University of Strasbourg to the *Parc de Orangerie,* which is situated across from the European Parliament, to protest the parliament's inaction to the social crisis being created by growing numbers of illegal Arab and black African migrants that had been flooding into Europe. Some of these well-behaved and unarmed marchers carried signs bearing such slogans as *European Whites Awake*! And *Who Speaks For The*

Rights of European Whites? Among the marches was a fair-haired young woman who was holding aloft a hand-made red flag upon which was sewn a stylized thunderbolt within a white circle. This evocative *Ring of Thunder* flag, as it would become popularly known, was later adopted as an official battle flag of the Movement.

As the procession began to cross the River Ill at the Pont d'Auvergne the heavily armed Senegalese troops, who had used their armored vehicles to form a barricade on the far side of the bridge, began to open fire without warning. The marshals at the head of the European column were cut down before they could signal the marchers behind them to halt. And then, as the survivors either threw themselves to the ground, or tried to flee the bridge, the mercenaries fired additional volleys point blank into the crowd. Many horrific images from the scene of this massacre had been captured on cell phones and were soon flooding the Internet....

On 13 October 2012 the Movement made its first coordinated leap into militant action. This was accomplished by a series of sequential events that had begun in Strasbourg with a rocket attack on the barracks of the Mobile Guard's Senegalese unit; another missile assault followed at the Mobile Guard headquarters in Paris; while in Brussels a car-bomb destroyed the façade of the secretariat building of the criminally incompetent European Union; in London a car bomb also exploded near the Parliament at Westminster; and several hours later, a powerful charge of explosives were set off at the entrance of the Old Customs House in New York. Responsibility for these initial acts of civil insurrection was claimed shortly thereafter with an announcement by the Movement....

By the early months of 2013 the militant action of 13 October 2012 had grown into a full-blown insurrection by anti-globalist forces in both Europe and America. Open warfare had broken out—and widening swaths of territory was being taken and held by fighting groups of revolutionaries. How did the globalist establishment answer this rising armed rebellion that was rapidly spreading on both sides of the Atlantic and threatening the very foundations of the global empire? The answer was with terror! Anti-globalist combatants were now declared to be lawless bandits and liable to immediate execution when captured. Legislation was also passed that legalized public executions. Two-story wooden gibbets, which could accommodate as many as eight hangings simultaneously were soon being constructed in so-called public spaces—plazas, etc.—of every city and town controlled by the globalists. However, few public hangings would ever take place on these scaffolds due to the immediate outcry of revulsion by the general public upon the first appearance of the gruesome, medieval structures, although most of them were left standing in their stark, unfinished condition as a grim warning—as a threat. And so it went, this cruel Civil War between the globalists and the anti-globalist Europeans....

Earlier in the War, before my first meeting with Nicholas Abelov in Bologna, and after his earliest victories in Ukraine and Crimea, he had had a dramatic military success during the winter of 2014-15 at the Tisza River in Ruthenia. It was there that he defeated an entire army group led by the formidable German General Rudolf von Rosenstein one of the most prominent of the globalist commanders. This victory at the Tisza River was a signal event in the growing wartime reputation of Nicholas Abelov. It also led him to a sequence of other military triumphs, the first of which took place toward the end of 2015 at the Po River in northern Italy, and was followed by two successful campaigns during 2016, first in the mountainous German south and then farther north where he liberated key German seaports along the contiguous coastlines of the Baltic and North seas—a final death blow to the empire's war-making ability in the strategically important north-central area of Europe's western peninsula. In addition, during this climatic period of the Civil War, Nicholas Abelov's numerous victories had literally transformed him into a folk hero for millions of anti-globalist European Whites....

On the dark, chill morning of 5 January 2017, the globalist empire's European leadership formally surrendered to anti-globalist forces in the snowy city of Brussels. Col. Nicholas Abelov had a leading role at the signing ceremony that was being televised from the now austere, formerly ornate, reception hall of the defunct European Union. Shortly thereafter, I received an e-mail from Nicholas Abelov wishing me good health for the coming year. He ended his New Year message with an account of an odd wartime incident:

One night after we occupied that part of the Baltic littoral west of Königsberg, the enemy began to bombard us with heavy artillery fire. During the bombardment I went outside to have a look around. What was I looking for? Was it my fate as a leader?

Some months following the story's telling, I concluded that—yes, Nicholas Abelov was probably testing his ultimate *fate* as a military leader when he deliberately exposed himself to the obvious dangers of an intense enemy artillery barrage. As a scholar of Nietzschean thought, Nicholas Abelov was surely familiar with the philosopher's imperative concerning the fitness of a leader:

[Y]ou must first be quite clear as to his prime physiological condition, a condition I choose to call great healthiness, which is not a mere static possession, but which he is constantly acquiring—and must acquire, because he is continually sacrificing it and must so sacrifice it!

PART TWO

Winter, an ill guest, sits in my house; my hands are blue from his friendly handshake. He is a hard guest, but I honor him, and do not pray to a fat-bellied fire-idol, as weaklings do.

Nietzsche—Thus Spoke Zarathustra

8

As one of the early members of the anti-globalist Movement and a grim witness to an almost unbearable display of human suffering that took place during the deadly wars of secession, I can still only grudgingly offer something like a nod of sympathetic understanding to those fellow anti-globalists, who for various reasons of their own, had become agnostic in the course of those bloody conflicts. On the other hand, during this persistently harsh winter, whenever I have viewed the mirage-like forms of the past wavering dimly in the gray receding distance, I am reminded of a short passage from Alain Badiou's *Being and Event,* which I have chosen to paraphrase here for my own purposes:

There is a certain element of the detective novel in the... enigma: an empty salon, a vase, a dark sea—what crime, what catastrophe, what enormous misadventure is indicated by these clues?

Raymond Chandler's exquisite literary studies of mid-twentieth-century Los Angeles were disguised as detective novels. Last night I added several partly coded lines to my evolving study of the Revolution, which is not disguised as a detective novel, but as a memoir that I continue to write despite a mocking comment attributed to Ernest Hemingway on the subject of personal journals:

Autobiography is the highest form of fiction.

Yesterday, when I went into The Summit Café for my usual afternoon cup of strong coffee and a long leisurely perusal of the English language newspapers, I discovered Dominic Putnam seated at one of the tables with a shiny new mechanical pencil and notebook lying in front of him. This was quite a surprise. I would have thought that by now he had already left Davos after his interview with me. Did he perhaps meet a young woman who was delaying his departure? I almost asked him this whimsically intrusive question point blank—however, he was anxious to tell me something else: that he had found another place to stay that was on the village side of the gushing mountain torrent and the wobbly wooden foot bridge. That was fine as far as it went, but it still did not explain what was keeping him in Davos after we had completed our discussion. I had a suspicion of what the reason might be, but I wanted to hear it from him. Yes, he finally admitted that he was now hoping to have another brief conversation with me on a subject that, regrettably, we had not reached in the earlier interview. Apparently, I was the only one among the founders of the Movement (that he was able to locate) who had also been a member of the Provisional Assembly when it held its contentious emergency session in Davos following the invasion of Poland by the Chinese. Would I possibly agree to another very short chat with him concerning this special session of the Provisional Assembly that had been held here at Davos, Switzerland in October 2019?

"Look, here" I said, a bit sharply," There is a virtual Tibetan mountain range of archival material readily available to history writers that addresses the meeting of the Provisional Assembly here at Davos in 2019."

"Yes, I know," he replied unperturbed, "but you are the only one among the founders who can still construct a lucid and savvy description of this Assembly session now almost twenty years in the past."

We finally agreed to meet again at The Summit Café in two days....

I had been a member of the Revolutionary Coordinating Council, as well as a delegate to the Assembly at the time of the ill conceived decision by the Speaker of the Assembly to temporarily abandon Brussels and hold an ad hoc session in the Swiss Alps. The idea of a Coordinating Council was born after the historic European Nationalist International held at Moscow early in April 2012. Following the Moscow conclave, members of the anti-globalist Movement immediately reassembled at Innsbruck, Austria to make plans for managing the European secessionist storm that was already beginning to gather on the horizon. When the storm struck early in 2013, the Coordinating Council took over as the temporary Executive branch of the Revolutionary Government, which then lacked a constitution. At the time of the Chinese invasion in 2019, the Council again became the de facto Executive arm of the Revolutionary Government still without a functioning constitution.

During the Civil War and then the Chinese invasion, as well as the brief period of fragile peace that was sandwiched between the two wars, the Revolutionary Coordinating Council was generally recognized as the intermediate guarantor of the new European State's continued existence. At the same time, however, petty self-aggrandizing satraps arose, fattened and multiplied within the querulous confines of the Provisional Assembly, and the Constitution remained unratified because the basic powers of the Revolutionary Government's Executive branch had not been clearly defined by the squabbling Assembly members....

9

After having agreed to meet Dominic Putnam again at The Summit Café two days hence, I spent part of the interval reviewing entries in my journal relative to events that occurred during the month of October 2019 (one of the most turbulent periods of the anti-globalist secession). Beyond the notorious 10-14 October meeting of the Provisional Assembly in Davos (upon which Dominic Putnam now seemed to be obsessing) other events of much greater import were also taking place during the same fateful month. For example, the following are several journal entries I made during that time:

9 October 2019

Immediately after the sudden death of the Revolutionary Coordinating Council's inaugural Director, the Prussian eagle Eugen von Oldenburg, in Brussels on 7 October, Bishop Oliver Dunhill was elected as his replacement. The Bishop is a brilliant, multi-lingual English cleric, who several years earlier had been relieved of his formal religious duties and eventually excommunicated by the Roman Curia because of his unwavering opposition to many of the ultra-liberal initiatives that had been adopted by the divisive Second Vatican Council. For instance, Bishop Dunhill has demanded an answer to this question: What has become of the two-thousand-year-old Christian imperative to convert the Jews? Today self-opinionated Rabbis of various unflattering descriptions are still routinely invited into the hallowed chambers of the Holy See and allowed to flaunt their contempt for the Church and the ineffable European Culture that the Church had created. And another related question: How will the Church withstand the deadly threat of the Islamic Jihad when its leadership fails even to mildly censure the disrespectful behavior of our traditional antagonists the Jews?

A second entry was made later the same evening of 9 Oct 2019 also relating to the election of Bishop Oliver Dunhill as the new Director of the Coordinating Council.

And so a changing of the guard has taken place in the Revolutionary Coordinating Council! Despite Bishop Dunhill's banishment by an obscure cabal of Vatican bureaucrats, and his down-playing of this drama by adopting an austere black uniform with molecule-size flashes of purple and a simple turned collar as his mock armor, this exiled Prince of the Church (who notably smokes Turkish cigarettes in a carved ivory holder) has now declared his unyielding intention to be just as fierce a defender of our social mythos, as he has been a defiant guardian of our ecclesiastical tradition. Still one wonders what immediate effect Bishop Dunhill will have on the Chinese that have driven through southern Russia and Ukraine and are now at the eastern edge of central Europe itself? It is my hope and belief that the new Director will make a bold stand to stem this Chinese tide—perhaps in the style of Pope Leo the Great who stopped the advance of Asian armies under Attila the Hun at Lake Garda before they were able to surge farther south to Rome….

24 October 2019

   I was just returning to Brussels after a fact-finding visit to the battlefront in eastern Poland, when I received word by phone that Bishop Dunhill wanted to see me.

   The Revolutionary Coordinating Council is currently located in a gray-tinted glass structure in Brussels' governmental quarter. The building was previously used to house several sections of the now defunct European Union's bureaucracy. From inside the dark-tinted glass façade of this ultra-modernist 20th century building the view is always the same: an eternally overcast Brussels....

When I entered Bishop Dunhill's office the new Director welcomed me with the sign of the cross, and then gestured to a leather side-chair facing his desk.

"What is happening in that beleaguered nation of Poland?" The Director asked.

"As we speak, a Chinese army is poised on the far bank of the Vistula River—across the river is Warsaw. There is a brave plan to defend the Polish capital—but, unfortunately, bravery is not always rewarded with success. I will have a complete written report for you shortly."

"Did you hear any talk of a coup d'état among our military?"

"I heard a lot of bellicose talk at the Vistula, but really nothing about an actual coup d'état— besides, what is there to overthrow here?"

"Our futile Provisional Assembly comes to mind...."

The plain-spoken, displaced Catholic Bishop seemed free and easy compared to his predecessor, the great Eugen von Oldenburg, whose commanding demeanor had stamped him with the regal traits of a sovereign bird of prey. I was quite at ease in the new

Director's company, despite the fact that we were discussing a possible military disaster in central Europe. At one point I even asked: "Would you prefer to be called Director or Bishop?"

"I do not see any need for formality," he answered. "We are all in the same boat, are we not? We are all revolutionaries fighting for a good cause, whose fate is still far from settled. I might have even suggested that we address each other with a simple word like comrade—had that word not been pirated and painted with the black brush of disrepute by its misuse in ultra-left political jargon. So in view of that and other considerations, I would simply say, use whatever is most natural—for example, my given name, as you know, is Oliver."

The Director then behaving in the manner of a sovereign Prince of the Church placed a Turkish cigarette in his carved ivory holder, and we resumed our discussion of the dark situation in Poland where Chinese forces were already threatening the very heart of Europe....

Finally he said: "It seems to me that we have reached a point in this uncertain conflict with the Chinese where a lucky soldier is needed—a lucky soldier who might also be a charismatic political leader."

I said nothing.

"Does that remark not carry the implicit

notion of a coup d'état?"

"Yes, I would say that it does," I declared, now openly reacting to the provocative nature of the Director's words.

"No one seems to know the whereabouts of Nicholas Abelov. There is a rumor that you and he sometimes exchange e-mail messages. Do you know where Nicholas Abelov is at the present time?"

"No, not at present," I replied, "but I will try to find out."

This could to be easier said than done in the developing chaos created by the Chinese invasion of the European peninsula....

10

When I met with Dominic Putnam at The Summit Café for a second interview in late February 2039, I was determined that the conversation would not extend past the agreed upon one hour, as had happened on the earlier occasion. And to lower his expectations, I immediately announced that nothing of real value, or even of serious interest had been produced at the Davos meeting of the Provisional Assembly in October 2019. And then, as if placing my judgment in a shatterproof capsule, I summed up the by saying: "This so-called emergency session of the Provisional Assembly had been an absolute waste of time."

Dominic Putnam calmly ignored my verdict. "It seems to me that the meeting held here in Davos succeeded in dramatizing the severity of the Chinese crisis, and thereby strengthened the resolve of Europeans to resist this threat to their beleaguered Nation."

It was obvious that this young "writer of political history" was determined to fashion a silk purse from a sow's ear. Dominic Putman was looking for heroes and heroic acts, but he was looking in the wrong place.

"The October 2019 meeting only highlighted two things: the enormous ineptitude and blatant corruption of the Assembly leadership," I said. "If you have not already done so, you should consult the records of the post-war corruption trial of this same Belgium Speaker of the Provisional Assembly, whose idea it was to hold an ad hoc session in Switzerland, and also the trials of his underlings in the Provisional Assembly! On 19 October 2019 the Polish capital of Warsaw fell after heroic resistance, and the entirety of central Europe lay open to the Chinese armies. The only thing that was brought to light at the Davos meeting was the desperate need for an heroic act to save the Nation! That heroic act did not come about during the calamitous, four-day meeting of the Provisional Assembly here in Davos—that heroic act occurred in the city of Brussels, where a successful coup d'état took place on 26 October 2019!"

Dominic Putnam glanced at me with a look of suppressed annoyance.

"I understand that you were involved in the coup d'état," he said.

"I had knowledge of the impending coup, but

I was not personally involved in its execution."

"It has been said that you were an important civilian figure who represented the Revolutionary Coordinating Council in organizing plans for the coup d'état."

"I was a temporary link between the civilian Revolutionary Coordinating Council and the military Defense Command during the Chinese emergency. Considering the state of affairs in the corrupt, barely functioning Assembly and the hard reality of Chinese armies on the loose in Central Europe—the situation cried out for swift, resolute action."

"It has been said that some members of the Revolutionary Coordinating Council were against supporting a coup d'état."

"There are always those who will object to the use of extra-judicial methods even during a life and death situation. This was a threat to the continued existence of a fledgling nation, not a summer shower that threatened a ladies lawn party...."

11

And now this meandering narrative has again circled back to the critical month of October 2019. Bishop Oliver Dunhill, the current Director of the Revolutionary Coordinating Council, had hinted that a coup d'état would probably be necessary if the new Nation was to be saved—he also mentioned the need for a lucky soldier and inquired about the present whereabouts of the missing Nicholas Abelov. I had told him that I did not know where Nicholas Abelov was at present, but offered to make an attempt to locate him (although I admitted to myself that finding Nicholas Abelov at a time when he had apparently chosen concealment, was not likely)....

I could no longer reach Nicholas Abelov on the Internet, nor at a phone number that he had once given me, so I attempted to contact a dependable member of the Provisional Assembly, who I thought might know how I could reach this "lucky soldier." The trustworthy member of the Provisional Assembly was Rolf Quintinius, a young Baltic German who served on the Assembly's Defense Committee, one of the few committees in this disreputable governmental body that was still more serious about defending the Revolution than it was about increasing its own political power base.

After discussing the dire military situation in eastern Poland with the new Director, I left his office and phoned Rolf Quintinius.

"Where are you at the present time, sir?" He asked.

"In the rotunda of the Assembly Hall," I told him.

"Don't move from the rotunda," he said. "I'll be right there."

It was now late afternoon, the domed rotunda of the elegant Assembly Hall was crowded and noisy. Glancing around, I accidently caught a glimpse of myself reflected in the mirrored dome. Was that really me up there? Well, yes, I could not deny it. A rather disheveled fellow wearing a khaki trench coat, whose various soldierly brass buckles did not conceal a bedraggled look after having been worn for almost a week on the muddy Polish battlefront. So, there I was reflected in the dome of the rotunda, a middle-aged European with a touch of gray at his temples, something that I had not noticed before, but which was now quite apparent in the rotunda's bright light.

The reflection of a fifty-year-old European White man with graying hair—still slim, some might even say gaunt. A professional revolutionary who did not wish to appear too well-fed when dealing with the usually indifferent, but sometimes the malign moods of History herself....

Then the *young* revolutionary Rolf Quintinius was there smiling warily (probably remembering that only moments earlier he had said to a founding member of the Movement, *"Don't move"*).

"I owe you a cup of coffee," I said. "Let's get out of this den of iniquity and find a café where we can talk."

We found a quiet café nearby.

Before I could ask him if he knew where Nicholas Abelov might be, he said: "Col. Abelov wants to see you."

"Where is he?" I asked, not bothering to point out the serendipitous nature of the situation.

"I'll take you there," he said.

Before we left the café, Rolf Quintinius made a short phone call:

"Sir, he has just returned from the warfront in Poland....Yes, we will be there immediately."

Our destination was a nondescript building at the former military complex of the defunct European Union. As we approached the building in the growing dusk, I had the intuitive sense that this apparently abandoned complex was now actually bristling with armed soldiers—perhaps elements of the elite Special Forces unit that only days before was being held in reserve at Strasbourg. The presence of such a unit would indicate two things: preparation for a coup d'état was now well underway and that the military was supporting it. An officer, actually wearing the insignia of that elite Special Forces unit, was waiting for us in front of the apparently abandoned building. He immediately escorted us inside, and then to a well-guarded conference room off the main lobby where Nicholas Abelov was seated at a table with nine other men (all of whom were dressed in civilian clothes). When we entered the room Nicholas Abelov rose to greet us—and then indicated with a friendly gesture that we should take seats.

I recognized several of those men at the table as officials, or former officials of the Revolutionary Government and others as ranking military officers—two members of this group of nine would soon be playing major roles in a post-coup government. One was Jack Thompson, a still youthful looking lawyer from Virginia who had served as chairman of the historic First Nationalist European International held at Moscow in April 2012—now in October 2019, a senior member of the Provisional Assembly in Brussels. The other figure at the table, who would also play an important role in the coup d'état, was the

Irish General Daniel Sullivan, Commander of the Revolutionary armies on the Continent. I had known General Sullivan since the first secessionist war when I was assigned to Military Command Headquarters as a civilian liaison from the Coordinating Council. General Sullivan appeared to be quite comfortable sitting there in a brown Irish tweed suit.

Col. Nicholas Abelov asked if I wished to make any remarks before the meeting proceeded. I identified myself as a member of the Coordinating Council, as well as the Provisional Assembly, and pointed out that the Council, the interim executive branch of the Revolutionary Government, was now headed by a new Director, who had only an hour or so earlier, after hearing my report on the desperate situation in eastern Poland, charged me with the task of locating Nicholas Abelov for the sole purpose of proposing to him that he lead a coup d'état to save the European Nation. With that short explanatory, some might say provocative, statement I again took my seat.

Jack Thompson then summarized the central elements of the agreement that had been adopted by this group at the meeting a short time before we had arrived:

The structure of governance following the coup d'état is to take the form of a Consulate. Three

Consuls will administer the Consulate. A Senate of Notables will be appointed by the Consuls as a deliberative body. The term of the Consulate would not exceed five years, it will be followed by popular elections.

On 26 October 2019 a bloodless coup d'état, a singular act to save the European Nation, took place shortly after dawn in Brussels with the full support of the military. Col. Nicholas Abelov, the coup leader and First Consul of a temporary governing Consulate, made a sequence of public appearances later that day wearing the plain yellowish-brown khaki uniform that he had famously worn during the Civil War, and whose only decoration remained the Ring of Thunder badge worn by all soldiers, regardless of rank, who had been in close combat with the enemy.

That evening Nicholas Abelov made a brief appearance on television from an office in the Provisional Government's Executive Headquarters, accompanied by the two other members of the ruling Consulate: General Daniel Sullivan then the Military Affairs Consul and Jack Thompson Consul for Civil Affairs. After introducing the two other Consuls, Nicholas Abelov announced that with the sole exception of the non-political Coordinating Council the Provisional Government had been dissolved.

"Henceforth, it will be the responsibility of

this three-member Consulate to navigate our new Nation to a safe harbor," declared the First Consul in closing.

Then just before midnight the three Consuls made a final public appearance at a torch-light rally of thousands in the largest square in Brussels. This was not a gathering of demoralized Europeans whose heartland was being threatened by foreign armies. It was a thrilling outdoor spectacle—a lively rally of free people, who were confident that they would successfully defend their new Nation....

12

In early November 2019, approximately two weeks after the fall of Warsaw, Generalissimo Chia Bong, Supreme Commander of globalist forces in Europe, resumed military operations in eastern Poland. Shortly thereafter, it became evident that instead of an expected massive thrust directly west from the center of the Chinese line, a strategy of limited scope was emerging. The main Chinese army group had now pivoted northward toward the Baltic littoral rather than due west toward the heart of Europe itself.

Apparently, faced with the imminent arrival of winter, the Generalissimo had opted to secure his line in the north at the Baltic Sea. His choice of the Baltic coast as the place to anchor the northern terminus of his winter line, a line that began at the great natural barrier of the Carpathian Mountains in the south, had the strategic advantage of depriving European forces of any further access to the strategic

Baltic area....

This then was the tactical thinking attributed to Generalissimo Chia Bong by the European military analysts in November 2019—and, as if to confirm their conclusions, Chinese troops quickly took the city of Konigsberg, the first of several important eastern Baltic ports, including Stettin (the German name), which would also fall to the Chinese shortly thereafter.

During this critical period of November 2019, a curious television report was beamed from Beijing as part of the coverage of fighting taking place along the Baltic littoral in the vicinity of Konigsberg. This mostly unnarrated account featured the appearance Generalissimo Chia Bong in Konigsberg. It began with a long shot of the Generalissimo emerging from a camouflaged staff car, which had stopped in front of the entrance of Konigsberg's ancient university. The time of day seemed to be early morning, a wet snow was falling. Generalissimo Chia Bong was wearing the formal uniform he wore only on special ceremonial occasions: a dove-gray greatcoat trimmed with flashes of scarlet and sapphire and a deep-blue visored cap bearing the Empire's new symbol, a Chinese serpent. The camera then followed the Generalissimo as he entered the venerable university, where he was shown walking slowly down dimly lit

corridors accompanied by a small military escort—
and finally into a lecture hall. There in this large,
unoccupied hall Generalissimo Chia Bong stood
apart from the others; his gaze sweeping across the
coffered ceiling, the high narrow windows, the empty
row upon row of wooden desks and benches worn
smooth and some disfigured by centuries of use.
Finally, his eyes came to rest upon a dais where a
lectern stood beneath its carved acoustical roof from
which the voices of countless scholars had been cast
into the echoing lecture hall. After a brief period of
meditation, the Generalissimo departed....

But why on that wintry November morning
did the Supreme Commander of the Empire's armies
in Europe visit an unoccupied lecture hall at
Konigsberg's university dressed in a formal uniform?
Presently a voice offered a non-specific explanation
of this unnarrated visit: "Generalissimo Chia Bong
wished to honor a learned scholar who once taught
there."

It was left for a loquacious Manchu adjutant
to first disclose the identity of the person who the
Generalissimo had wished to honor by visiting the
university in Konigsberg.

"Do you know the name Immanuel Kant?"
Generalissimo Chia Bong had asked the unfortunate
adjutant.

"Generalissimo, I am sorry to say, that I do

not know that name." replied the ram-rod straight Manchu adjutant with an unsoldierly stammer.

"Immanuel Kant was a German philosopher who lectured at the university here in Konigsberg," declared the Generalissimo. "He is the author of a famous maxim that you should study:

So act that you could will the maxim of your action to be a universal law."

13

As many of us in the northern hemisphere still remember, the snow began to fly in December of 2019. Record snowfalls and arctic temperatures were experienced throughout the entire region. However, these extreme conditions would soon be used as an advantage by Col. Nicholas Abelov the chief military strategist, as well as First Consul of the beleaguered European Nation.

What follows are excerpts taken from reports compiled at the end of the European counteroffensive conducted against the Chinese that commenced on Christmas Eve 2019.

This compendium describes the European campaign that began along the northern flank of the battlefront on 24 December 2019 and concluded with the surrender of all Chinese forces in Europe on 11 February 2020.

Two hours before daybreak on 24 December

a newly arrived American Special Forces brigade, supported by German armored elements, broke through the enemy lines at Stettin, overrunning surprised units of the crack Chinese 9th Dismounted Cavalry (read assault infantry) Division that had earlier cut off land access to the city. The dramatic sundering of the Chinese iron ring around Stettin ripped loose the anchor that had been holding most of the Chinese northern flank in place. Following the rout of the Chinese 9th Division, the attacking forces quickly turned the northern right flank of the Chinese line. European armor then followed the break-through at Stettin by driving eastward to retake the other Baltic cities beyond, including Konigsberg, after which it wheeled south into the interior of eastern Poland toward the strategic Vistula and Warta rivers—and eventually cut off the Empire's forward Command Headquarters at Warsaw. In the meantime, the Chinese line on the central front began to crumble like a plaster wall in an earthquake. To the south additional European military elements, consisting of several battle-hardened Slavic armored brigades, had skirted the north-eastern slopes of the Carpathian Mountains, and were already driving northward into the wide open flatlands of south eastern Poland….

In January 2020, after the fortunes of war had

turned irreversibly in Europe's favor, a televised news bulletin beamed from Beijing announced the combat death of Generalissimo Chia Bong.

The Commander has fallen at the front while directing attempts to relieve his troops holding out in the city of Konigsberg....

What follows is a conclusion to the summary of reports describing the European counteroffensive that ended with the defeat of all Chinese forces early in 2020. These excerpts resume with the death of the Chinese Generalissimo.

There was extensive television coverage of the farewell ceremonies held for Generalissimo Chia Bong at an airstrip somewhere near the Polish capital. A guard of honor and muffled martial music accompanied the flag-draped coffin as it was carried across the wet tarmac and placed aboard a military aircraft. Television cameras then followed the flight of the lone plane as it flew eastward into China. Soon it was seen flying over very mountainous country illumined by a dramatic sunset. Lofty mountain peaks floated on oceans of cloud and were bathed in colors from roseate to pale sapphire, while funereal music continued in the background and the reverential voice of a narrator identified this magnificent mountain scenery as that of old Szechwan Provence, home of the fallen Generalissimo—and the fiery face of a peak towering above all the others as the majestic peak of Minya Konka. But what of the Generalissimo's successor? General Ye Ho, the new Chinese Supreme Commander, was quickly shown to be no match for the First Consul as a military strategist, nor was he the equal of the new European Commander, the German-Huguenot General Felix LeTour. By the last week of January most elements of the Chinese military presence in Central Europe had been effectively trapped in an iron net. To the east, guerrilla units in Russia and Ukraine, reorganized earlier by Nicholas Abelov, had now completely severed the Chinese supply lines and were attacking the enemy's rear. In Poland, which was still the main theater of operations, European troops from the north and south had joined with the newly reinforced center, and were drawing a bristling seine purse ever tighter around the main Chinese force. Finally, during the first days of February, European forces won two decisive battles. One of these took place at the medieval capital of Krakow; the other was fought at a strategic point on the Bystzyca River near the city of Lubin. On 11 February, a gray rainy day, the counterinsurgency campaign directed from Beijing came to an end. The new commander of Empire forces in Europe signed surrender documents that day at a rural railroad station just west of Warsaw. Television coverage was permitted at this historic event. News cameras were even allowed inside the rather ramshackle stucco station itself during the formal surrender. General Felix LeTour and members of his staff had arrived first and were already seated on one side of a long wooden table when a small party representing the defeated Chinese forces arrived. This was the first time the world had glimpsed the new Chinese Supreme Commander. General Ye Ho was not dressed in the striking ceremonial uniform of a Commander of Empire Forces, as Generalissimo Chia Bong had been when he visited Immanuel Kant's lecture hall at the university in Konigsberg: (the dove-gray coat trimmed with flashes of scarlet and sapphire, and a deep blue visored cap). Now the new Chinese Commander, a man short and slim, was wearing the conventional Chinese peppermint green field coat and a black metal helmet. However, what was quite remarkable about the general's appearance as he entered the shabby station, what immediately caught the attention of millions of viewers watching this momentous event on world wide television, was a close-up of Ye Ho's bright-red mustache, probably inherited from an ancestral member of a tribe of redheaded Huns....

PART THREE

Great star! What would your happiness be, if you had not those for whom you shine?

Nietzsche—Thus Spoke Zarathustra

14

So here we are again in the current year of 2039, which still includes the lingering presence in Davos of Dominic Putnam. Yes, Dominic Putnam had remained in Switzerland following the second interview in The Summit Café. *Skulking about* is not the right term to describe the young man's behavior during his extended sojourn in Davos, nor does the equally pejorative term *lurking* or *prowling about* accurately describe his later days in Davos. No, Dominic Putnam was, to put it in plain English, just *there*. When I occasionally observed him walking through the wintry streets of the village with his ever-present notebook, I was sometimes tempted to invite him to The Summit Café for a warm drink—but then, after taking a second look at that over-sized notebook tucked under his arm, I would manage to resist the impulse.

Instead, I began to develop an imaginary storyline that attempted to explain Dominic Putnam's oddly enduring presence in Davos—the scenario could have been called:

The Secret Life of Dominic Putnam

This pastime soon became boring, however, so I abandoned it and looked around for some other mountain peak to climb....

Then one blustery afternoon at the end of February, when the wind was whistling through the mountain passes, I spied Dominic Putnam taking shelter in a doorway, and invited him to join me for a cup of coffee —he accepted.

Once we were seated in the cheery confines of The Summit Café, I asked him a direct question: "Have you established permanent residency here in this dull little town?"

"Oh, no," he said with some amusement, "but the bracing mountain air has caused me to linger here longer than I had planned."

"What have you been doing since we last talked?"

"I have been thinking."

"Thinking?"

"Yes."

"About what?"

"The Revolution!" he replied "I have been reviewing the statements that were made to me by the

Movement's founders, before I finally sit down and begin to write."

"How many of the founders were you able to find? "

"Only about a dozen—and that includes you, of course. The years, as well as the wars, have taken their toll...."

I made no comment.

"In reviewing my notes I found that your name was mentioned quite frequently...."

I said nothing.

"You have a *reputation*," Dominic Putnam said, "which indicates to me that much of your story has been told by others."

I remained silent.

"This might also explain why parts of your story continue to puzzle me."

Then I spoke: "You have what you have," I said, not unkindly.

"Yes, I *do* have what I have," he cheerfully agreed, then he asked, "Do you know the name Francisco Luis de Madrid?"

I gestured with open hands indicating that I did not know the name....

"Francisco Luis de Madrid is an Argentinean historian and a daring literary innovator," Dominic Putnam said. "For example, he suggests that a writer of history should be free to insert fictional characters into his narrative, if by so doing the writer enhanced the clarity of what might otherwise remain a clouded, or incomplete factual situation...."

I wondered about this Argentinean historian, and his notion that history writers should be free to mix fact with fiction. Was Dominic Putnam signaling to me that he might use fictional stand-ins to shed light on certain aspects of my role in the Revolution that he found puzzling?

I agreed to meet with him again at The Summit Café two days hence....

When we met again Dominic Putnam asked me about a car bombing that had occurred in the city of Zurich. The incident occurred in early 2020, when we were still at war with the Chinese in Poland. Dominic Putnam had not asked me about this event before.

"What makes you think that I would want to talk about the Zurich bombing now?" I said a bit grumpily.

"The bombing was a devastating event," he said. "You were severely injured by the blast. I thought you might want to make some personal comments about it."

"The Zurich car bombing," I said, "occurred in January 2020, shortly before Nicholas Abelov's defeat of the Chinese armies in Poland. The bombing had apparently been an isolated act of terrorism possibly perpetrated by members of the Islamic Caliphate, or even by some disgruntled European globalists. No one ever took responsibility for the blast—so it might have been just a stupid mistake. In any event, a meeting had been held in Zurich that day, which included several members of the Revolutionary Coordinating Council who were there to arbitrate a jurisdictional dispute over rights to post-war waterways in north-western Europe. This seemingly complicated issue was resolved rather quickly, however, and the meeting ended much earlier than was expected. The three members of the Coordinating Council then left the hotel conference room to be driven back to the airport. Two of the three entered a waiting car in front of the hotel. I was not with them at that moment because I had left my cell phone on a table in the conference room. After retrieving the phone I immediately left the hotel. The two other members of our party were already in the waiting car. As I exited the hotel lobby and was approaching the car, an ear-splitting roar took place, The car in which I was to have joined my two colleagues had exploded, it had literally disintegrated in a great fireball! I was thrown to the ground amid the burning debris....

"Let's say I was pretty well smashed up by the bomb blast—a bloody sack of broken bones was rushed to a Zurich hospital and promptly wrapped from top to bottom in a plaster cast. After a rather extended period I was finally released from the hospital and transferred to a sanitarium here in Davos for further treatment. Sometime later, I was invited to stay temporarily at the mountain villa of an elderly member of the Austrian nobility who did her best to spoil me with kindness, while the sanitarium was being transformed into an apartment complex, where I have since made my home...."

"One of the founders suggested that you were somehow involved in carrying out the car bombing," Dominic Putnam said, consulting a page in his notebook.

"Yes, I know exactly who you are referring to," I said. "He was one of the few individuals who supported Lorenz Ehrenstaat in the doctrinal dispute that was debated at Lubeck in 2014. This individual, who I will not dignify by using his name, had earlier held me reasonable for Lorenz Ehrenstaat's suicide, which followed shortly after the debate. Now, years later, he obsessively accused me on the Internet of having been behind the 2020 Zurich car bombing. Why? Because one of my colleagues, who was tragically killed in the car blast, had also supported Lorenz Ehrenstaat at the time of the 2014 debate. I answered this public attack by inviting my accuser to visit me here in Davos where the matter of the car bombing could be discussed privately, unsurprisingly he has yet to arrive...."

15

Dominic Putnam finally left Davos—finally left my mountain stronghold and descended to the flatlands again—still unarmed, still without even the small pistol, whose ivory handle had been decorated with a houndstooth checkered design, the diminutive gun that I now capriciously imagined was given to me by the young woman who would later become the mother of Dominic Putnam—this deadly little pistol that neither of us had ever mentioned in any of our conversations, but which was perhaps the totem-like object that had dwelt at the very center of Dominic Putnam's particular interest in my personal story of the Revolution....

Many transforming events had taken place since the beginning of the anti-globalist Movement early in the twenty-first century. The specific period spanning the years from the coup of 2019 to the years immediately following the establishment of the Consulate is illustrative. What follows is a list of the most significant events of that period. After the coup d'état, the governing Consulate headed by Nicholas Abelov defeated the Chinese armies in Poland, ending the so-called War of 2019. Following that victory the three–chambered Consulate began to utilize what remained of its five-year period of political power to strengthen the structure of the new European Nation. At the end of the Consulate's rule, elections were promptly held on both sides of the north Atlantic; these elections produced an utterly transformed National Assembly; the formerly interim Senate of Notables was then institutionalized as a permanent ninety member deliberative body to advise the Legislative and Executive arms of government in lieu of a national judiciary; adequate powers were also awarded to the formerly toothless Executive; and formative elements of a Constitution were debated, some were adopted, others were not; finally an awe-inspiring replica of the original Roman Republic's Constitution was submitted to the Assembly for its approval; this Constitution of the new Nation was ratified by acclamation. What was the immediate practical consequence of all this? The European race now faced its most implacable enemy, the Arab Islamic Caliphate, stronger and more united than it had ever been before....

Over the years I have been both blessed and cursed. I have had abysmal luck and amazingly good fortune. For a long period of time I had need of a silver knobbed walking stick to get me from place to place. I can still remember standing at the French doors of the Countess's mountain villa wondering if I would ever walk again without the aid of her late husband's silver knobbed cane. Now in 2039 I am standing in my apartment looking down on the snowy rooftops of Davos. The scene below is certainly not as operatically dramatic as was the view of the snow-covered mountain peaks outside the Countess's villa, but since leaving there I have received an unforeseen blessing—the silver knobbed cane now shares space in my ceramic camel umbrella-stand, unneeded and unused....

Today I was literally blessed with another letter from Bishop Oliver Dunhill. We have now become correspondents—yes, letter writers, since we have found ourselves more, or less marooned outside the mainstream of revolutionary politics. For me it was after being smacked by a car bomb blast. In the case of the intrepid Bishop it was since he resigned as Director of the Coordinating Council, following ratification of the new Constitution. At that time the Director had on several occasions referred to the once vital Revolutionary Coordinating Council as *a social club for old men*. Bishop Dunhill remains an impatient man, despite the fact that he is now seventy-five, exactly five years my senior, and occasionally suffers from gout.

The following is taken from Bishop Dunhill's latest astonishing letter:

We are living in a time and in a place that could be hell, or a neighborhood that is close to hell. This means the Devil is now our neighbor, as well as being the masked Emperor of Tolerance. The tyranny of Tolerance has made everything possible. The Emperor of Tolerance is now loved and feared by all. Tolerance has made the Devil our most famous Superhero! And if you do not believe that, then look at our White culture today. It is a shambles. It has become a laughing stock. It is a social and moral joke. Less than a life-time ago the word "White" was synonymous with "Christian." Now our magnificent cathedrals and churches are empty, or they have become Muslim mosques. The once all-powerful Vatican is now reluctant to criticize even the most arrogant and disrespectful Jew or Muslim. And now can it be that this great Church, this great White Church, turns its back on its besieged members? There was a time when the Church was fearless, when the Church preached against the most vile of sins—when the fearless Church was not loath to condemn the practice of human sacrifice—yes, human sacrifice! When the fearless Church did not turn its back on those living in the neighborhoods nearest to hell! Now a priest of the ancient Coptic Church, the earliest of Christian Churches, a Church whose early members remembered seeing the Christ walking, smiling, gesturing—an Aryan Church that recognizes the Bishop of Rome as its father, asked for help from a village outside of Marrakesh. I found the appeal on the Internet. I switched off my computer with dismay! Then, as quickly, I turned it on again and made a reservation for a flight to Casablanca. I landed in Casablanca early in the evening. I was disoriented by the noise and the dazzling lights. For a moment I feared that I might die in Morocco. I hired a cab driven by a young man who seemed to have an honest face. I asked him why he drove a cab. "So that I can become a lawyer," he said. I asked him where I could buy a gun. He drove into the Casbah, and we found a weapons shop. I bought an old French army revolver and a box of ammunition. We found the village at the edge of a dry riverbed. A village elder was waiting for us in front of a white-washed stucco church. The cab driver acted as an interpreter. The village elder made the sign of the cross and then said that their priest was dead. He pointed past the dry riverbed and toward a row of low hillocks that were silhouetted against the sinking red sun. We followed the old man across the dry riverbed—and then, as we approached the hillocks, we saw the dead priest. This was not Hollywood! The priest was nailed to a cross!

We took the priest's body down from the cross. Then, as I did what is spiritually required for a Christian burial, the old man and the cab driver went back to get shovels. We buried the dead priest's body. We knocked down the cross, which no longer resembled a cross, and tossed the rough pieces of sun-bleached wood, into the dry river bed. Then we returned to the village where the other villagers had come out of hiding. They stood silently in front of the little white-washed church: mostly old woman and young children, a few young women, a few old men. It was hard to look at them. The cab driver spoke briefly to the villagers in their native tongue, a young lawyer taking his first pro bono case. I blessed each of them, kissed each on the cheek. Later, as we drove back to Casablanca, I thought of the times when the Church was great because it was fearless! I thought of the times in the past when the Church would enter the dark neighborhoods of hell to say, No! That is greatness— that is fearlessness!....

A second letter was delivered to me along with the one from Bishop Dunhill. This letter was in a pale lavender envelope. It was a small stationery-size envelope like those sold boxed with note paper of a matching color. I had put it aside to first read Bishop Dunhill's thundering letter. When I finished reading the Bishop's letter, I picked up the lavender envelope, but did not open it. There are times when our intuition says, "No! Don't go there." This was only a commonplace piece of mail. Still it was not quite the same as a semi–anonymous throwaway advertisement. It presented itself as a personal letter. On the upper left-hand corner of the envelope was a number, probably an apartment number, "24". Under that was a street address and then a city, Lubeck....

I put the envelope down again. For some reason I did not want to touch it. It was as if by touching it I was committing a transgression of some kind. I was also still shaken by Bishop Dunhill's shattering letter. My hands were still trembling. I looked at the inexpensive little envelope lying there on my writing table. Somehow it looked cold, it seemed as if it was shivering with cold, or with fear. Then I tried to imagine what might be inside the envelope. It would probably be a single page note written in a woman's hand, as were the addresses on the envelope. I did not know a woman in Lubeck. I then tried to think of what she might have written:

Hello. You do not know me. I was not made famous by anything I did during the anti-globalist Revolution. However, I am pleased to say that I know you. I began to follow your career as a revolutionary leader after hearing your debate here at Lubeck in 2014. That debate made you a popular figure—and made me an ardent anti-globalist. I am now the mother of a twenty-six-year-old writer who, as you know, has been gathering material for a book on the founders of the anti-globalist Movement. Yes, you know my dear son Dominic Putnam because you graciously allowed him to interview you on several occasions. As Dominic's mother, I would like to thank you for being so generous with your time. Also I am a little curious about the fate of a small pistol with a bone handle that was given to you by a smitten young woman at the beginning of the Civil War. It was one of a pair of dueling pistols that had belonged to her paternal grandfather. I will end this note by extending an invitation to you for a dinner of dol bot (a native Himalayan stew) should you ever visit Lubeck.

I then picked up the small lavender envelope again and carefully tore it in two.

Afterword

This political trilogy was written as a warning: something of great weight and bulk is hurtling at break-neck speed toward us. This is not the cartoon cliché of a large piano, or a safe falling out of a window. Our culture is a shambles. And now our race, our last refuge, our final line of resistance, is under assault. "Stop!" That is what the anonymous Narrator of this third book said before the novel began. He was among the first to see the galloping advance of a runaway horse named Destruction. He became one of the early founders of the anti-globalist Movement. Now at the age of seventy, he calls himself "an old man." He carries wounds both visible and hidden, but he still walks two miles each day to stay reasonably fit. His narration of *The Wars & Other Related Events* is his memoir, *it will be* his only monument.

R.M.W.

Notes

Abelov, Nicholas, a brilliant young Russian military commander and European folk hero, who led an anti-globalist army to a major victory over Empire forces at the Tisza River in Ruthenia.

Anonymous Narrator, one of the founders of the anti-globalist Movement, who as an "old man" of seventy is writing a memoir.

Austrian Countess, who invited the Narrator to stay at her Alpine villa when he was recovering from a bomb blast.

Bong, Chia, a Chinese Generalissimo, who was Commander of Chinese Empire forces during the invasion of Europe during the War of 2019.

Clausewitz, Karl von, Prussian general and military historian: "War is politics by other means."

Dunhill, Oliver, an English Roman Catholic Bishop expelled from the clergy because he dissented from varies positions adopted by the Church at the Second Vatican Council.

Ehrenstaat, Lorenz, a founding member of the anti-globalist Movement who debated an important ideological issue with the Narrator at Lubeck in 2014. Shortly afterward he committed suicide.

Khazars, a Turkic tribe that in the Middle Ages adopted Judaism as its religion. After the Chinese invasion of eastern Europe in 2019 the Khazars attempted to gain control of the waterways in south-western Russia.

Leo I, a Pope who was called the Great. He saved Rome by persuading Attila leader of the Hunnish armies not to invade Italy.

Madrid, Francisco Luis de, an unconventional historian and literary innovator who maintained that historians should be free to use fictional characters in their narratives, if by so doing the writer enhanced the clarity of what would otherwise be a clouded factual account.

Nietzsche, Friedrich. What has not been said of this scapegoat, this martyr? He called himself the *good European*! Nicholas Abelov called him the great redefiner of our vocabulary.

Putnam, Dominic, a young historian who has been interviewing the surviving founders of the anti-globalist Movement in preparation for writing a history of their Revolution.

Quintinius, Rolf, a member of the Assembly and also its Defense Committee. His meticulously kept journal during the Revolution became a vital part of the archive that was compiled for the previous book of the trilogy *The Revolt Against Empire*. *In the final book of the trilogy this true European patriot appeared in only one scene—a sad commentary on the fleeting nature of fiction, as well as of life.*

Sullivan, Daniel and Thompson, Jack. These two members of the anti-globalist Movement played prominent roles in the coup d'état of 2019 led by Nicholas Abelov. They both became part of a three-member consulate under Col. Abelov that would save the new Nation.

Wittgenstein, Ludwig, a theorist of language whose poetic sensibility allowed him to delve deeply into the mysteries of words. He ended his only work *Tractatus Logico-Philosophicus* with this: *Whereof one cannot speak, thereof one must be silent.*

Ye Ho assumed command of Chinese forces in Europe after the death of Generalissimo Chia Bong in Poland. Ye Ho was a slightly built, unassuming figure when he appeared at the surrender ceremony in his peppermint green field coat and black metal helmet. There was, however, one aspect of appearance that drew attention, his very bright red mustache.